First Facts®

Underground Safari

ROOTS, BULBS, AND BACTERIA
GROWTHS OF THE UNDERGROUND

by Jody Sullivan Rake

Consultant:
William D. Bowman, PhD
Professor, Department of Ecology and Evolutionary Biology
University of Colorado
Boulder, Colorado

CAPSTONE PRESS
a capstone imprint

First Facts are published by Capstone Press,
1710 Roe Crest Drive, North Mankato, Minnesota 56003
www.capstonepub.com

Library of Congress Cataloging-in-Publication Data
Rake, Jody Sullivan, author.
 Roots, bulbs, and bacteria : growths of the underground / by Jody Sullivan Rake.
    pages cm. — (First facts. Underground safari)
 Summary: "Teaches readers about plants, plant parts, and other organisms that grow and live underground"—
Provided by publisher.
 Includes bibliographical references and index.
 ISBN 978-1-4914-5062-8 (library binding)
 ISBN 978-1-4914-5092-5 (eBook pdf)
1. Roots (Botany)—Juvenile literature. 2. Plant anatomy—Juvenile literature. 3. Soils—Juvenile literature. I. Title.
 QK644.R27 2016
 581.4'98—dc23
                          2015000104

Editorial Credits
Abby Colich, editor; Heidi Thompson, designer; Jo Miller, media researcher Katy LaVigne, production specialist

Photo Credits
Alamy: Nigel Cattlin, 9; Newscom: Mark & Audrey Gibson Stock Connection Worldwide, 21, Photoshot/NHPA/Joe Blossom, 7; Science Source: Martin Oeggerli, 19, Nigel Cattlin, 13; Shutterstock: Alexander Raths, cover (right), itman_47, 15, IVL, 2-3, Jiri Vaclavek, 5, Julie Clopper, cover (middle), KRUKAO, cover (background), 1, 2-3, Iuri, 17, Mirko Rosenau, 8, pzAxe, cover (left), Showcake, 5, Swapan Photography, 10, yuris, 11

Design Elements
Shutterstock: Hal_P, LudmilaM

Printed in China by Nordica
0415/CA21500544
042015   008845NORDF15

yellow onions

TABLE OF CONTENTS

DOWN TO EARTH

The world is full of plants. Some are tall trees. Some are tiny weeds. Almost all plants have parts that grow under the ground. Underground plant parts include *roots* and *bulbs*. Plant parts grow underground to reach the soil. Plants need soil to grow.

root—the part of a plant that is underground
bulb—an underground stem from which a plant grows

roots ▼

roots ▲

5

GIVE A HOOT FOR ROOTS

When a seed is planted, it starts to
sprout. *Shoots* sprout above the ground.
Roots sprout below the ground. Roots have
two jobs. They keep the plant firmly in
the ground. Roots also soak up water and
nutrients from the soil to feed the plant.

sprout—to start to grow
shoot—plant part that is beginning to grow above ground
nutrient—a substance needed by a living thing to stay healthy

shoot ▶

DIG IN!

Roots are good for soil too. During heavy rain, roots keep soil from washing away.

◀ roots

VEGGIES IN THE GROUND

Some roots become wide and large. Large roots store vitamins and *carbohydrates*. We eat some of these roots as vegetables. Root vegetables include carrots, beets, and radishes.

carrots ▲

carbohydrate—a nutrient that provides energy

Before refrigerators people kept food in underground storage areas called root cellars. During winter months, root vegetables stayed fresh in root cellars.

▲ radishes

WHAT'S THAT SMELL?

A bulb is an underground stem. Roots and shoots grow from the bulb. Many thin layers of plant leaves make up bulbs. They have a strong smell. Some flowers, such as tulips, grow from bulbs. Onions, garlic, leeks, and other vegetables are bulbs.

onion bulb ▶

▼ **garlic bulbs**

11

NO SMALL POTATOES

A tuber is a thick part of the stem that grows underground. Roots grow from the tuber. Tubers store water and energy to help the plant survive dry seasons. Some tubers can be food for people. Potatoes are a type of tuber.

DIG IN!

Potatoes are a popular food. In 2012 Americans ate about 106 billion potatoes. That's about 340 potatoes per person!

◀ potatoes

13

SEEDS IN A POD

A legume is a plant that grows *pods*. A pod is a group of seeds wrapped in a little package. Peas and soybeans come from pods. One legume's pods grow underground. When its seeds are mashed, they make a tasty sandwich spread. Can you guess what it is? Peanuts!

pod—a long case that holds the seeds of certain plants, such as peas

DIG IN! Peanuts are not really nuts. Most nuts grow on trees. Peanuts are named for peas, their legume relatives.

◄ **peanuts**

FUNGUS AMONG US

Fungus is not a plant. It is not green and has no stems, leaves, or roots. But it is an *organism* that grows out of the ground. Mushrooms are a fungus. One type of mushroom grows underground. It is called a truffle.

DIG IN!

Truffles are a pricey menu item. This is because they are hard to find. People who hunt truffles use dogs and pigs to sniff them out!

organism—a living thing such as a plant, animal, bacterium, or fungus

▼ truffle

17

TINY GARDEN LIFE

Millions of tiny organisms live in soil. They are too small for you to see. *Bacteria* and other *microbes* feed on dead plants and animals. They leave behind nutrients. The nutrients help *fertilize* the soil. They make the soil better for growing plants.

bacteria—very small living things that exist everywhere in nature
microbe—a tiny living thing that is too small to see without a microscope
fertilize—to make soil rich and healthy

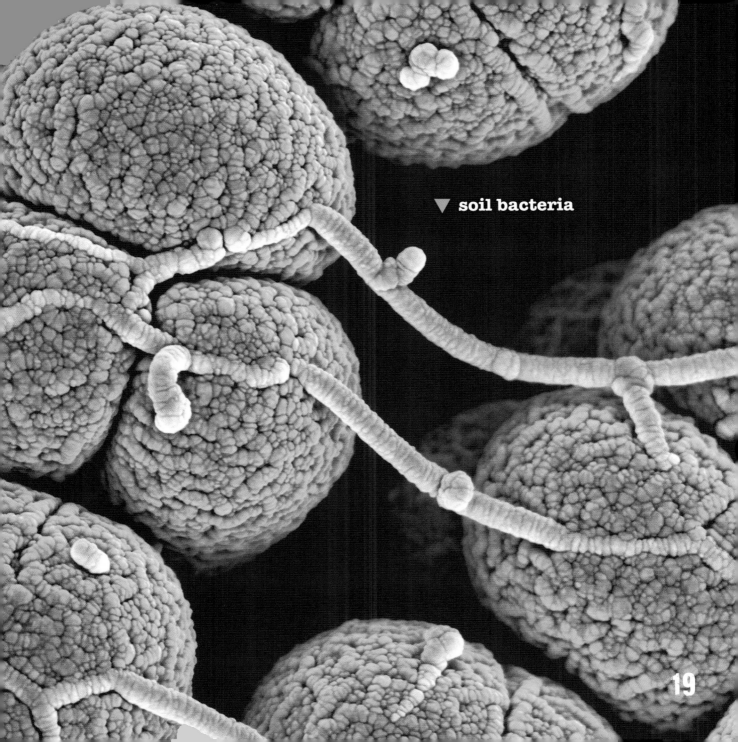

soil bacteria

19

GROWING PLANTS FOR LIFE

Plants provide food for people and animals. Taking care of them is important. Farmers use *pesticides* to protect plants from bugs. But too many pesticides harm the *environment*. The environment is our home, and plants are our food. We need to take care of both!

pesticide—a poisonous chemical used to kill insects, rats, and fungus

environment—the natural world of the land, water, and air

DIG IN!

Plants and soil feed each other. They pass nutrients back and forth. Farmers plant different crops each season. Switching crops provides many different nutrients to the soil.

GLOSSARY

bacteria (bak-TEER-ee-uh)—very small living things that exist everywhere in nature

bulb (BULB)—an underground stem from which a plant grows

carbohydrate (kahr-boh-HY-drayt)—a nutrient that provides energy

environment (in-VY-ruhn-muhnt)—the natural world of the land, water, and air

fertilize (FUHR-tuh-lyz)—to make soil rich and healthy

microbe (MYE-krobe)—a tiny living thing that is too small to see without a microscope

nutrient (NOO-tree-uhnt)—a substance needed by a living thing to stay healthy

organism (OR-guh-niz-uhm)—a living thing such as a plant, animal, bacterium, or fungus

pesticide (PEST-uh-side)—a poisonous chemical used to kill insects, rats, and fungus

pod (POD)—a long case that holds the seeds of certain plants, such as peas

root (ROOT)—the part of a plant that is underground

shoot (SHEWT)—plant part that is beginning to grow aboveground

sprout (SPROWT)—to start to grow

READ MORE

Aloian, Molly. *What are Bulbs and Roots?* New York: Crabtree Pub. Company, 2012.

Lynette, Rachel. *The Science Behind Plants*. Chicago: Raintree, 2012.

Waldron, Melanie. *Roots*. Plant Parts. Chicago: Raintree, 2014.

INTERNET SITES

FactHound offers a safe, fun way to find Internet sites related to this book. All of the sites on FactHound have been researched by our staff.

Here's all you do:

Visit *www.facthound.com*

Type in this code: 9781491450628

Check out projects, games and lots more at
www.capstonekids.com

CRITICAL THINKING USING THE COMMON CORE

1. Explain why plants need soil. Explain how plants are good for soil. (Key Idea and Details)

2. Reread pages 10 and 12. How are bulbs and tubers alike? How are they different? (Craft and Structure)

3. What would happen if a plant did not have roots? What are other ways a plant could get the nutrients it needs? Support your answer. (Integration of Knowledge and Ideas)

INDEX